This book belongs to

Bridget

Contents

Tiger clouds	3
Mess? What mess?	11
Just look at that!	19
We like colours	27

Information pullout

New words	32
Learning to read with this book	34
Read with Ladybird	36

Cover illustration by Sumiko Davies
Illustrations on pages 32-33 by Peter Stevenson

A catalogue record for this book is available from the British Library

Published by Ladybird Books Ltd
A subsidiary of the Penguin Group
A Pearson Company
© LADYBIRD BOOKS LTD MCMXCVII

LADYBIRD and the device of a Ladybird are trademarks of
Ladybird Books Ltd Loughborough Leicestershire UK

All rights reserved. No part of this publication may be reproduced, stored in a retrieval system, or transmitted in any form or by any means, electronic, mechanical, photocopying, recording or otherwise, without the prior consent of the copyright owner.

Tiger clouds

written by Catriona Macgregor
illustrated by Sumiko Davies

It looks just like a tiger.

Now it looks just like a bear.

Now it looks just like a monster.

Now it looks just like a bird.

Now it looks just like a face.

Now it looks like rain.

Mess?
What mess?

written by Shirley Jackson
illustrated by David Pattison

I like helping...

Don't make a mess.

I like mixing…

Don't make a mess.

I like pouring...

Don't make a mess.

I like tasting...

Don't make a mess.

I like baking...

Don't make a mess.

I like eating...

Don't make a mess.

Mess? What mess?

Just look at that!

written by Shirley Jackson
illustrated by John Dillow

Just look at that!

Just look at that!

Just look at that!

Just look at that!

What a good party.

We like colours

written by Catriona Macgregor
illustrated by Tania Hurt-Newton

He likes blue and

she likes yellow.

He likes red and

she likes green.

He likes pink and

she likes brown.

But **I** like them **all**!

New words introduced in this book

baking   eating   helping

mixing   pouring   tasting

brown   green   blue

all, but, he, looks,

Just look at that!

All the words used in this story have already been met in earlier books in the series. Join in together with the speech bubbles. Encourage your child to read this story with expression. The exclamation mark after 'Just look at that!' shows your child that a loud and lively voice should be used.

We like colours

This short story introduces your child to reading several colours and the pronouns 'he' and 'she'. What is your child's favourite colour?

New words

These are the words that help to tell the stories and rhymes in this book. Try looking through the book together to find some of the words again. (Vocabulary used in the titles of the stories and rhymes is not listed.)

Read with Ladybird...

is specially designed to help your child learn to read. It will complement all the methods used in schools.

Parents took part in extensive research to ensure that **Read with Ladybird** would help your child to:

- take the first steps in reading
- improve early reading progress
- gain confidence in new-found abilities.

The research highlighted that the most important qualities in helping children to read were that:

- books should be fun – children have enough 'hard work' at school
- books should be colourful and exciting
- stories should be up to date and about everyday experiences
- repetition and rhyme are especially important in boosting a child's reading ability.

The stories and rhymes introduce the 100 words most frequently used in reading and writing.

These 100 key words actually make up half the words we use in speech and reading.

The three levels of **Read with Ladybird** consist of 22 books, taking your child from two words per page to 600-word stories.

Read with Ladybird will help your child to master the basic reading skills so vital in everyday life.

Ladybird have successfully published reading schemes and programmes for the last 50 years. Using this experience and the latest research, **Read with Ladybird** has been produced to give all children the head start they deserve.